Library and Archives Canada Cataloguing in Publication

Title: TA-DA! : a story of egg donation / written by Ella Kay ; illustrated by Farida Zaman.
Names: Kay, Ella (Children's author), author. | Zaman, Farida, illustrator.
Identifiers: Canadiana (print) 20220193096 | Canadiana (ebook) 2022019310X |
   ISBN 9781772602470 (hardcover) | ISBN 9781772602487 (EPUB)
Subjects: LCSH: Children of egg donors—Juvenile literature. | LCSH: Egg donors—
   Juvenile literature. | LCSH: Fertilization in vitro, Human—Juvenile literature.
Classification: LCC RG135 .K39 2022 | DDC j618.1/780599—dc23

Editor: Kathryn Cole

Printed and bound in Canada

*Second Story Press gratefully acknowledges the support of the Ontario Arts Council
and the Canada Council for the Arts for our publishing program. We acknowledge the
financial support of the Government of Canada through the Canada Book Fund.*

ONTARIO ARTS COUNCIL
CONSEIL DES ARTS DE L'ONTARIO
an Ontario government agency
un organisme du gouvernement de l'Ontario

Conseil des Arts   Canada Counc
du Canada   for the Arts

Funded by the Government of Canada
Financé par le gouvernement du Canada

Published by
Second Story Press
20 Maud Street, Suite 401
Toronto, Ontario, Canada
M5V 2M5
www.secondstorypress.ca

TA-DA!

A Story of Egg Donation

written by Ella Kay
illustrated by Farida Zaman

Second Story Press

Mama, Dada, tell me again how I was made.

Well, a long time ago, before you were born, Dada and I fell in love.

Life was great. But we asked, "What could make it better?"

And the answer was you!

But *how* did you make me?

When a sperm mixes with an egg,
it creates a teeny version of you.
That's how babies are made.

We tried very hard.
We wanted you so much!

We tried....

And we tried....

But it didn't happen.

We felt
very sad.

So, what did you do?

We learned that there are people who donate eggs and sperm to help other people make a baby.

A doctor mixed Dada's sperm with a donated egg and put them inside of me.

And it worked! We were so excited when you started to grow!

You stayed inside my tummy for 1, 2, 3, 4, 5, 6, 7, 8, 9 months—such a long time!

I got so big,
I waddled!

You got so long,
your foot kicked my belly!

And when you had grown big and strong enough, you were born.

And
TA-DA!
Here I am!

Here you are!
You make us so happy.
We can't imagine life without YOU!

Ella Kay is the mother of two small children and lives in Toronto, Canada. *TA-DA!* is her first children's book. She wrote it to tell her children the story of "how" they were made.

Farida Zaman is the author of *I Want to Be...A Gutsy Girls' ABC* and the illustrator of many children's books, including *When Mom's Away*, which she co-created with her daughter. She works from her home studio in Toronto.

Dedicated to Ari Baratz and the entire Create Fertility team. Your tireless commitment enables dreams to come true; families all over the world are forever grateful. And to Kateryna, for giving us the gift of life, twice.

– E.K.

To all the healthcare workers.

– F.Z.